McCall Collection of Modern Art

David and Napoleonic Painting

Published by Fratelli Fabbri Editori,
Publishers, Milan, Italy, and

The McCall Publishing Company
New York, New York

Illustrations Copyright ©1970, in Italy,
by Fratelli Fabbri Editori, Milan, Italy

PUBLISHED IN ITALY UNDER THE TITLE
Mensile d'Arte
ALL RIGHTS RESERVED. PRINTED IN ITALY
Library of Congress Catalog Card Number: 72-122489
SBN 8415–1017–2

Introduction

One century before a young Corsican upstart burst dramatically on the scene in late eighteenth-century France, Louis XIV had sponsored a unique campaign of self-propaganda. By marshaling an army of artists and artisans to do his bidding under the supervision of his minister Colbert and the painter Charles Le Brun, he saw to it that his personal exploits were infused with a noble, heroic aura and widely heralded. But with the eclipse of the Sun King's grandeur, neither the French Court, which had patronized various forms of art, nor Louis XV and Louis XVI, his two successors to the throne, were able to create a *modus vivendi* or a distinct artistic style to pivot around the reigning monarch, except for the two decades during which Madame Pompadour set the tone for all Paris.

With the rise of Napoleon, official art patronage took on renewed vigor. Bonaparte commanded a publicity system already perfected under the Revolution; moreover he had first-rate men at his disposal to carry out his wishes. He fully recognized the utility of art as a political instrument adapted to his personal service. With scrupulous care he examined every painting and every item of furniture destined for his various palaces or for transference to one or another city of his realm. By no means unschooled, in some of his letters he revealed himself a true connoisseur and a man of taste in such subtle, comparatively trifling matters. Whether he was scanning the details of the master plan for a battle campaign — of which, we hardly need point out, he invariably emerged the hero — or choosing the colors of a tapestry, he promptly imposed his own personality and exerted so strong an influence on art and current fashions that we cannot mention the Empire style without calling up his image in our minds. This is, indeed, one of his rightful claims to glory.

For the most part, his ideas derived from common sense. Deft and sure, he could often sniff the danger of a banal emphasis or some vulgar adulation, hence adverse propaganda, and avoid it. The artists in his service could not always give his single feats a triumphant splendor, nevertheless David, Gros, Girodet, Gérard, Prud'hon, Ingres, and Géricault left masterpieces that would have been inconceivable without Napoleon and the society he created.

This confirms our contention: that art can indeed fulfill a propaganda mission. It is not the subject itself that conditions the validity of a painting, as the

1

examples reproduced in this volume amply testify, but the manner of its presentation and the creative form the artist has adopted to interpret it. Is *Guernica* a masterpiece? And what else if not a propaganda pamphlet, an *engagée* painting, as it would be termed today? Indeed, if the artist is unequal to the task, his canvas will be a fiasco, but so it would be too if he attempted no more than the portrayal of a pretty young girl. A painter must find the subject matter best suited to his talents. Can we imagine battles depicted by Prud'hon? They would be only flower battles. But during the Empire no one ever assigned him such subjects, and Napoleon, who much admired his art, commissioned him to execute works suited only to his special aesthetic sense.

Gros, on the other hand, was most eloquent in his representations of Napoleonic warfare; lacking this stimulus in later years, his art declined to insignificance.

Napoleon taught David a good lesson on at least one occasion. When the young general was crossing the Alps, the artist insisted that he pose at length so that his portrait could be finished. "It is not," the general pointed out, "an exact duplication of features, a small mole on the nose, that constitutes a likeness. No one asks if portraits of great men are accurate likenesses. The one essential thing is to recognize their genius." To be sure, we do not much care today whether that sublime canvas portrays Bonaparte in precise detail or not; what matters is that we see the youthful hero as an ambassador of the revolution that proclaimed its message of freedom far beyond the confines of his country, and we are convinced of his romantic idealism.

Other works, however, were not always of comparable quality. For example, Gautherot depicted *Napoleon Wounded Before Ratisbon* in an inferior painting exhibited at the 1810 Salon. Only a foot was wounded, and the heroic possibilities of a foot are limited even if, as the tactful Denon wrote, "the great merit of this composition lies in the fact that it focuses on a single interesting action wholly concentrated on the person of Your Majesty. The entire Army thinks of nothing but you, Sire, and you think of nothing but the Army's anxiety." Elsewhere Denon declared that "there are no unrewarding subjects in painting except to those without genius or energy," a valid viewpoint, but everything has its limits.

The Salon of 1810 was a veritable anthology of Napoleonic exploits and anecdotes, including such important works as David's *The Distribution of the Eagles,* Girodet's *The Revolt of Cairo,* and Gros' *The Taking of Madrid,* plus others, now forgotten, that fell into a cloying, irksome sentimentality. Boisfremont's *The Emperor's Clemency*—toward the Princess von Hatzfeld, whose husband, the civil governor of Berlin, was charged with treason—hardly moves us despite her dramatic gesture; *Napoleon's Clemency Toward Mademoiselle Saint-Simon Asking Pardon for Her Father,* by Charles Lefond "le jeune," is conceived with mawkish pathos; likewise Schnetz's *Death of General Colbert,* who utters these pompous words as he yields his soul to his Maker, "My death befits a soldier of the Grand Army because, as I die, I behold the last of my country's eternal enemies in flight."

More sophisticated are the subjects assigned to Berthon: *The Emperor Receiving the Queen of Prussia at Tilsit;* to Madame Auzou: *Arrival of the Empress in the Gallery of Compiègne Palace,* in which Marie Louise, flanked by her august consort, graciously receives floral homages from young girls; and to Menjaud: *The Empress Portraying the Emperor.* An exotic touch is supplied by Mulard in his *The Emperor Receiving the Persian Ambassador Mirza in the Finkestein Headquarters,* while Bourgeois serves up another tragic subject, *The Duke of Montebello's Last Moments.* To complete this parade of emotions and passions were two paintings, neither very successful, *The Battle of Austerlitz* and *His Majesty Addressing the Army Before the Battle of the Pyramids,* by Gérard and Gros respectively.

In the same year the decennial prizes, conferred by the Emperor to honor his outstanding artists, were awarded. We need not list here all the historical and mythological works on his list but only those illustrating a subject that, as they were then labeled, "brings honor to the nation's pride": *The Coronation of Napoleon in Notre-Dame* by David; *The Emperor Visiting the Enemy Wounded* by Debret; *The Emperor Addressing His Troops* by Gautherot; *The Emperor Receiving the Keys of Vienna* by Girodet; *The Plague of Jaffa, Napoleon on the Battlefield of Eylau,* and *The Battle of Abukir* by Gros; *The Soldiers of the Seventy-Sixth Regiment Retrieve Their Standards in Innsbruck* by Meynier; *The Revolt of Cairo* by Guérin; *St. Bernard Pass,* by Thévenin; and Charles Vernet's *Morning of the Battle of Austerlitz.* As we can see, Napoleon appears as protagonist in all of these eleven works except two: Gros' *Battle of Abukir* and Meynier's *Seventy-Sixth Regiment.*

By now the Napoleonic legend had become reality throughout the world, a goal the Emperor had pursued with astonishing, tireless persistence, subjecting not only himself but his family as well to an iron discipline. In March, 1807, he wrote this admonition to Josephine, "Greatness has its inconveniences; an Empress may not do what is permitted an ordinary woman."

But Napoleon's propaganda campaign was beset by one innate danger— compelled to exalt his actions, even the finest artists in his service were occasionally persuaded to distort truth into guises that strike us today as rhetorical and servile. In *The Taking of Madrid* (Plate 42), a work of many merits, Gros had to avoid any trace of controversy and interpret the conquest of the city as a liberation. The Spanish envoys, almost in tears, pray to Napoleon as if in the presence of a god. What really took place we do not know, but such an attitude would hardly have tallied with the surly mood of the proud Spanish people. Hence, reality was magnified, mythicized, warped, and, worse yet, violated in its very essence, which explains why this formidable painting is so rarely remembered today. Another painting familiar to everyone, *The Massacre of the Third of May* (Plate 43), by Francisco Goya, tells us the stark, historical truth of the events that occurred. The Goya work is one of the culminating achievements of nineteenth-century painting not only because of the originality and potency of the ideas it expresses but particularly because of the reaction it provoked when the spurting blood of the despot's victims brought wrathful censure down on his head.

Napoleonic art did not always stoop to compromises or accommodating absurdities; and even if, as that repentant revolutionary Quatremère de Quincy derisively wrote, it "was forced to lug its brushes around in the wake of the armies, to drag itself across battlefields, to traverse trenches and steppes, in short to chase after victory from the cataracts of the Nile to the mouth of the Oder," it often did so with nobility, grandeur, and sometimes with genius.

Portraiture

French painting in the Napoleonic epoch undoubtedly found one of its most fortunate manifestations in portraiture. David, foremost artist of the time, heir to the French portrait tradition of the *grand siècle* and the early eighteenth century, not only proved himself vastly gifted in this form of expression but, what is more, fostered a brilliant host of pupils who followed in his footsteps. To be sure, Napoleonic portraiture was inevitably panegyrical and seldom immune from that element of adulation characteristic of this art form to a greater or lesser degree in every age. Yet, by inflating its models with strong doses of vigor, grandiosity, and elegance, it gave posterity unforgettable images of a complacent, somewhat presumptuous society tinged with a faint but indelible shadow of vulgarity (Plates 15 and 23).

The ranking dignitaries of the Empire and the members of the reigning family were not always ideal models for an art with courtly pretensions. Not even the ultrasophisticated Robert Lefèvre could transform Madame Letizia (Plate 11), with her hard, coarse features, into the pale, aristocratic lady he would have liked to paint with something of a Van Dyke touch. Despite the frippery of her toilette, the luxurious furnishings around her, and the theatrical background, her expression is still sullen and stamped with that plebeian wisdom that so intimidated her son the Emperor. And what can we say of the insipid Marie Louise? (Plate 8) It would require even more than the skill, however awesome, of an artist like Gérard to endow her with a queenly, mysterious air. Only Canova, in his famous bust of her at Parma, could produce a convincing portrait that, incidentally, displeased his contemporaries because he had neglected to idealize the Empress.

On the other hand, Napoleon himself, at least in his youth, had physical traits that readily lent themselves to a credible eroticism. Young General Bonaparte made a powerful impression on the supreme French artist. "Oh, my friends, what a fine head! It is pure, it is grand, it is as beautiful as the ancients!...Here is a man to whom altars would have been consecrated in the classic times!...Bonaparte is my hero!" Thus did David describe the victor of

4

the Italian campaign to his pupils; and with the same sweeping fervor he painted the engaging sketch now in the Louvre (Plate 3), intended as part of a large composition to show him stipulating the peace treaty. Napoleon conceded one three-hour studio sitting for this work, which David never finished; only the head was delineated and later reduced in size. David's pupil, Delécluze, who was present at the sitting, reported that Napoleon "wore a simple blue redingote with a high collar that stressed his thin, yellowish face, rendered the more handsome by the artificial play of light that set off his prominent, well-marked features." Imbued with romantic ardor, his observation suggests the atmosphere that prevailed when Napoleon's first commissions were being executed—an atmosphere steeped in a literary exaltation that time had not yet quenched; our conclusion is confirmed by this work and others of approximately the same period. By comparison with Gros' freer and more frankly romantic *Napoleon at the Battle of Arcola* (Plate 2), David's painting displays more classic restraint, even if the same climate of poetic acclaim prevails; and we can discern a sense of Republican chauvinism and pride that still survived in France at the end of the century when Napoleon personified the nation's dream of glory, not yet faded.

Even when an Italian, the Lombard Andrea Appiani, portrayed the young hero (in a painting in Lord Rosebury's collection, unavailable for this volume but published by Hugh Honour in reproduction in *Apollo*, September, 1964), the features share something of the same elation. But Appiani gave his composition a more academic, *démodé* effect by including a figure of unabashed Baroque derivation (Victory holding the conqueror's shield); furthermore, the contrast between Bonaparte's modern uniform and the classical nudity of the winged figure seems today like an unintended note of satire. Soon after, David painted a portrait in which the general was depicted, according to his instructions, on a fiery steed, calm and serene, lifting one arm; he carries no weapon because that would hardly have been calculated to win people's hearts. Granted that this superb work (Plate 1) falls into rhetoric—the names of Napoleon, Charlemagne, and Hannibal carved on rock, the horse's melodramatic rearing—still we cannot agree with those who dismiss the work as cold and without vitality. This portrait, which is unquestionably Baroque in feeling, created a new type of heroic image, purposely avoiding any irrelevancy, with every non-essential element eliminated. If the political implications in the work have often been denounced, that is no longer of interest to us; such attacks are more justifiably directed to an altogether different kind of painting, Ingres' overwhelming *Napoleon I* (Plate 6). A concept of power so blatantly medieval, even neo-Byzantine, as this disquieting portrait proposes, could hardly have failed to dismay the democratic avant-garde of late eighteenth-century romanticism. But here, too, if we put aside outmoded politico-religious prejudices and look carefully, that sacred image emerges as a soaring paean to terrestrial power. As for its purely graphic values, we must go back to the subtlest refinements of the early Flemish to find examples of comparable skill. It is interesting to match this portrait with the small oil sketch David had executed the year before (Plate 7). Not even the Empire's most eminent artist arrived at Ingres' outright deification; in his imperial robes and surrounded by pomp, his Napoleon, even though invested with supreme power, is still a man. This applies likewise to Appiani's portrait commemorating Napoleon's coronation in Milan (the Vienna version of this work is reproduced here, Plate 9).

Ingres, however, was not always committed to this sort of representation. Several years previously he had portrayed the then First Consul in the quiet of his studio (Plate 4), intent on the cares of the state as custodian of the people's welfare. This image of Bonaparte won his special affection and gave him enduring gratification. He was also delighted with David's portrait of him in his studio (Plate 5), weary but alert after a sleepless night of hard work. Commissioned by Count Douglas, an Englishman who revered Bonaparte, this painting revealed the man in a new light, no longer at the threshold of absolute power as in Ingres' Liège painting, but now at the apex of his glory. Nevertheless, we are far from the heroics of *Napoleon Crossing the Alps*. Here we find a more human, realistic presence better suited to the needs of the moment, flaunting those virtues of understanding, benevolence, and compassion that the Emperor sought to advertise to the world.

Prud'hon "is the Boucher, the Watteau of our times. He errs, but not everyone may err as he does." David's viewpoint, at once stern and approving, touches on the most salient aspects of this early nineteenth-century artist's work. Prud'hon's art appears well removed from the contemporary mainstream; he seems to dwell in another climate, aptly defined by Delécluze as "an atmosphere of love." His impeccable taste, his delicate, morbid moods, his poetic fervor mark him both as the last exponent of eighteenth-century grace and the first interpreter of romantic melancholia. His *Portrait of the Empress Josephine* (Plate 13), for example, stylishly fuses these two elements. The figure is set against a landscape that in a sense, becomes the painting's real protagonist, imprisoning the lady's reverie in the humid atmosphere of the confining woodland. Compare this shadowy figuration of the Empress with Gros' posthumous portrait of *Cristina Boyer*, Lucien Bonaparte's first wife (Plate 12). Certainly there are similarities to Prud'hon's canvas—the graceful pose, the garden in the background—but the contrasts are more evident. Although they share a wistful mood, the Gros portrait is more alive and vigorous and suggests a more credible human being. Instead of Leonardesque fussiness over minute blades of grass and tiny flowers, Gros gives us a more honest study taken directly from nature, which he employs as an idyllic, scenic backdrop. Prud'hon's love of nature, of its mysterious, ethereal emanations, is even more apparent in his disturbing portrait *The King of Rome*, in which the young boy seems to have fallen under a spell, as if the encroaching vegetation had insinuated its magic powers into him. The artist's attributes, delicate and feminine in certain respects, attracted the Emperor's two wives—first Josephine, for whom he de-

6

signed exquisite decorations and other objects in the Bonapartes' *hotel particulier* in the Rue Chantereine; then Marie Louise, whose drawing master he became. He also designed enchanting items of furniture for the second Empress and painted a masterpiece, *Venus and Adonis* (Plate 60), now in London, which she forgot to acquire after it had been exhibited at the 1812 Salon.

Let us now examine another more intimate aspect of Napoleonic portraiture. While the Emperor preferred to be painted in his royal robes (except for some charming miniatures, such as one of Isabey's, published in *Connaissance des Arts,* November, 1966, page 85), the members of the family sometimes liked to pose in humbler attitudes. Note, for example, the lovely but rather foolish guise of *Queen Caroline as a Neapolitan Peasant Woman* (Plate 18) and the dual portrait of the Princesses Zenaide and Carlotta (Plate 19), executed by David in 1820 in Brussels. There are three versions of this work, but the only autographic one belongs to the Roccagiovine family in Rome; since it is unavailable, the copy in the Napoleonic Museum, painted in collaboration with his pupils, is reproduced here. This is a splendidly glazed, almost stridently polychromatic work typical of the artist's Belgian period. Clasped in a tender embrace, the two ungainly princesses gape at us as though frightened, stiff and anything but regal despite the crowns on their pretty curls and the imperial bees shown on the upholstery of the sofa. About to read a letter from their father, Joseph, exiled in Philadelphia, they try in vain to pique our curiosity. We could name other works of the same sort, but we prefer to pass over them and mention only the family's custom, borrowed from an old Bourbonic tradition, of decorating boxes and snuffboxes with portraits of themselves to give as gifts to friends and relatives. They even had themselves eternalized on fragile Sèvres and Neapolitan porcelain, as did the vain Murat (Plate 58).

Another contemporary classification of portraiture, often at cross purposes with the official current, focused on eminent figures who opposed the regime. When Madame Elisabeth Vigée-Lebrun returned to France after spending long years in pilgrimages to the courts of Europe, she was still loyal to the *ancien régime* and to those openly antagonistic to the Empire. In Switzerland she portrayed Madame de Staël, the new Caesar's obdurate adversary, as the authoress' own heroine Corinne (Plate 24). But the painter's once subtle, lyrical vein, too strongly identified with the vanished *douceur de vivre* to adapt to current trends, had by now almost ebbed away into sterility, and her pathetic efforts to convert from Louis XVI art to Empire neoclassicism came to nothing more than a diligent mediocrity. Several years later she struck a truly grotesque note in a latter-day Assumption, with Marie Antoinette awaited in heaven by Louis XVI and the unhappy Dauphin, both garbed for the occasion as unlikely cherubs.

An important work, however, is Girodet's portrait of the writer Chateaubriand (Plate 25), who complained that "under the Empire we all vanished. No more mention was made of us. Everything belonged to Bonaparte alone." This lament explains his dark mood and Napoleon's low esteem of him. "He's like a conspirator who has fallen down the chimney," the Emperor scoffed as he studied the canvas (now in the St. Malo Museum). Nor was he altogether mistaken. Indeed, Girodet had wondrously caught the complex, tormented character of the great author and produced a truly poetic physical and spiritual presence, using elements that were to become representative of romantic portraiture — the tousled hair, the dreaming figure, ancient ruins dotting the landscape, and a poignancy that also marks another portrait by Girodet of Baron Larrey (Plate 20). Although he respected the historical premises followed by other artists of his generation, Girodet introduced a genre of portraiture that anticipated future developments. He made no attempt to set the current style, as did François Gérard, the most elegant and fashionable, if not the greatest, portrait painter of his day (Plates 8, 15, and 16).

We conclude our brief review of Napoleonic portraiture with a comment on Gros' *Embarkation of the Duchess of Angoulême* (Plate 26), which, in a strict sense, does not belong in this category. One of the artist's last works, the crowded canvas depicts the daughter of Louis XVI (the only real man of the family, according to Napoleon) as she is about to flee France during the One Hundred Days. For his overall design, Gros borrowed all the devices of the great Baroque tradition but superimposed an operatic, nineteenth-century romantic mood. We seem to be watching the concluding scene of a melodrama, with the leading soprano singing her final aria while the other characters and the entire chorus listen in grief and dismay. The spectator's eye is irresistibly drawn to the unforgettable figure of the Duchess, with her sorrowful farewell expression somewhat alleviated by the richness of her dress and heraldic plume she energetically waves.

Ceremonial Painting

To represent Napoleon's coronation in Notre Dame in December, 1804, Delécluze tells us that David announced he wanted to do a portrait composition. Although he took many suggestions from Baroque art, particularly Rubens' magnificent series on Maria de' Medici, there were actually no traditional precedents to which he could refer; in a certain sense he foresaw such art forms as photography and the cinema. In conceiving his cycle, however, Rubens had leaned heavily on allegory, employing it as a device to transfer reality to a mythical plane. David, on the contrary, re-created his scene objectively as he himself, a most astute observer, witnessed it. With no gods or fabulous creatures on hand, the painting faithfully represents a specific historical ceremony (Plate 27) with meticulous accuracy of detail, with a spirit and chromatic richness that show David's immense gift for this genre. It has often been said that he felt the need to examine Rubens series not only to assimilate the laws of that master's prodigious world of composition but also to familiarize himself with his style and the bold, florid brushstrokes he used. The *Coronation* is indeed painted with an exuberance hardly to be expected from the sparing colorist of *Marat Assassinated* or *Napoleon Crossing the Alps,* done only a few years before. Now we can better understand David's role as master of that brilliant colorist Gros unless, as some maintain, it was the pupil who unwittingly imposed his influence on the master.

With due authority, the *Coronation* took a preeminent position in contemporary European painting and laid the groundwork for all future ceremonial painting of the century. It is fascinating to detect elements in this masterpiece that remind us of that other towering genius of the times, Francisco Goya. For example, the figures surrounding Madame Mère, the Emperor's mother, in the background (Plate 28) recall such Goya paintings as *La Junta de las Filipinas* (in the Castres Museum), but we emphatically disagree with those who insist that David was superficial while Goya was profound. Originally, David intended to portray the moment when Napoleon placed the crown on his head after wrenching it from the hands of the Pope, summoned from Rome for the occasion, but beyond doubt the Emperor adjudged this gesture too aggressive to be immortalized on canvas. Hence David was probably given the order to depict the action immediately following, when Napoleon lifted the crown over Josephine as she modestly bowed her head. "Fine, excellent, David! You have penetrated my thought to its very depths, you have made a French knight of me. I am grateful to you for bequeathing to the coming centuries the proof of my devotion to the woman who shares the burden of government with me," the Emperor exclaimed when he viewed the finished work. This outburst, spoken in public for public consumption, could only have been a calculated formality inasmuch as Bonaparte must have known every detail of the composition in advance; we are too well informed of the close attention he paid to each particular of those art works in which he figured, or which he commissioned, to doubt that David's choice of subject was made at the Emperor's bidding. In executing the *Coronation* and *The Distribution of the Eagles* (Plates 32 and 33) in the same series, David duly respected the precept, "Interest the spectator but without sacrificing everything to dramatic effect, as artists have done since the seventeenth century. Rather attract his attention to each figure in turn through the perfection of the treatment you give him." Thus, he was primarily concerned with minute detail, drawing innumerable studies of each character portrayed in these works as well as exhaustive sketches of the whole. Four paintings were planned for the series, the two mentioned plus *Napoleon Enthroned in Notre Dame* and *Napoleon's Arrival at the Hôtel de Ville* (the sketch is reproduced in Plate 30), neither realized because of political unrest. As if celebrating the life of a saint, the series was designed to pay tribute to Napoleon's civic-political career by representing four memorable episodes from it. The same scheme was simultaneously adopted, with even closer attention, to commemorate his military career.

The Distribution of the Eagles, now in the Versailles Museum, is likely to dis-

9

appoint the spectator for the lack of balance in its composition, but we cannot accuse the artist. Centered in the sky, which is neutral, David had planned to install an imposing winged Victory tossing leaves and garlands on the men below, but Napoleon almost certainly protested the intrusion of this unwanted, conventional figure in a work meant exclusively to extol his glory; thus he alone should appear distributing the rewards. David was consequently obliged to suppress his Victory and, in the process, sacrifice harmony of form. His original idea is preserved for us in the final sketch (Plate 31) now in the Louvre. All the same, this vast painting is still an artistic triumph. Not everyone will approve the attitude of the princes and marshals as they crowd around the Emperor and salute him with an excess of zeal (Plate 32), which inevitably recalls a like deference to more recent dictators, yet we cannot but admire the explosive, upsweeping rhythm of the mass of soldiers as they rejoice over the eagles and banners they have just received from their adored leader (Plate 33). Meanwhile, the group of princesses and courtiers, beautifully assembled between the towering columns in the background, is executed with a deft touch and a charming, chromatic delicacy that again reminds us of Goya.

Allegory

In their peculiar situation, David and his fellow court propagandists might easily have abandoned all caution and, in their intoxication, turned to allegory, if not outright deification; and indeed this is exactly what happened. One of the most unabashed yet successful examples of this development is a painting by Appiani, which was in the Royal Palace in Milan (Plate 55) until it was destroyed during the Second World War. Appiani had painted Napoleon's most crucial battles in monochrome; now he undertook a glorification of the Emperor in full color, showing him on an ancient throne supported by radiant winged victories and surrounded by guardian spirits offering him crowns. His noble torso is nude, his head is girt with laurel, and he holds the scepter in one hand and rests the other on a globe. In such unrealistic fantasies, the artist would sometimes introduce mythological beings to lend greater emphasis to his assumption theme. We know, however, that Napoleon disliked this sort of tribute and preferred a truer, more earthbound representation of himself. It was probably for this same reason that he never permitted Canova's statue of him to be exhibited in public; totally nude, the figure was eroticized not as a man of his own times but as an ancient, godlike emperor. Even in works that eulogized him with immoderate zest, he insisted on being portrayed in modern dress as, for example, he wished to appear with Marie Louise and the King of Rome in a work projected for the cupola of the Panthéon in a distinguished company of kings and saints from French history (see Gros' sketch, possibly done in collaboration with his pupils, in the Carnavalet Museum, Plate 53). Leafing through Salon catalogues of Bonaparte's time, we find few allegorical or mythological subjects; apotheosis had to be rooted firmly in reality, however blown up and legendized. Not until the Second Empire would we find another Napoleon to compare with Ingres' figuration, painted for the Emperor's Salon in the Hôtel de Ville, of which only a sketch survives today (Plate 52). Ingres presents him nude and valiant in a chariot drawn by four spanking steeds, crowned by Glory and preceded by Fame as he flies toward the empyrean over the head of France, crying hosanna.

Battle Paintings

By an odd paradox, Napoleon's first commission for a painting on a war theme described an encounter he did not command, *The Battle of Nazareth*, brilliantly led by General Junot. Bonaparte wanted the painting for his own collection and summoned the youthful Gros to execute it. Gros prepared a rapid sketch (Plate 34) so charged with fire, blood, and passion that nothing like it had ever before been seen in French art. The work was never realized, possibly because a fit of Napoleonic jealousy ended the project. The sketch, however, promptly won David's exceptional disciple another important commission for a work to commemorate General Bonaparte's visit to plague-stricken Jaffa during the Egyptian campaign. Exploiting the city's colorful setting in *The Plague at Jaffa* (Plate 40), the artist introduces a motley blend of oriental costumes and gives free rein to an exotic imagination, thus inspiring later works of Delacroix and other romantic painters. In this representation we see Napoleon, like a saint performing miracles, lightly tap the bubo of a plague victim while the terrified members of his retinue cover their faces with handkerchiefs or try in vain to deter him from this rash gesture. According to one witness, however, Napoleon never touched a single invalid; he merely strode rapidly through their midst and held a corpse momentarily in his arms. Moreover, the room in which this occurred was small and without a view of the city. In the action described by Gros, which, we must remember, meekly followed the instructions issued by Denon and therefore by Napoleon himself, we are asked to believe that the general's touch healed the sick, as Walter Friedländer pointed out. Thus, according to an ancient tradition that endowed kings with the gift of medical magic (Louis XVI was the last to preside over a session of such miracles), superhuman powers were attributed to him. Of greater importance, however, is the fact that in this work Gros gave us a hitherto unknown but wholly convincing facet of Napoleon's character and, at the same time, created one of the most original works of the epoch. Furthermore, it was the prototype of a genre that was to enjoy considerable success in nineteenth-century painting, paving the way for August Macke's Tunisian fantasies and Picasso's variations on Delacroix's *Women of Algiers.*

The image of a bold, generous, and merciful Bonaparte was then widely diffused. A curious example is Colson's mediocre canvas (Plate 44) in which the young general extends his right arm over the heads of two women in suitable Turkish garb kneeling beside his restive horse; both are weeping desperately as one holds a trembling infant aloft. In a gesture worthy of Solomon, with the same poise that marks so many of his contemporary portraits, Napoleon commands a soldier to sheathe his glinting sword. The painter missed no opportunities in setting his drama against an exotic oriental background and made the most of contrasting sartorial styles and attitudes.

Napoleon again posed as a wonder-healer, this time visiting the wounded on the island of Lobau, in a painting by Charles Meynier (Plate 41). Without a colorful Eastern setting or bizarre costumes to help him, Meynier had to content himself with an imposing, somewhat desolate landscape and a pontoon bridge in the distance. To enhance his effect, he pointed up the decorations on the military uniforms and yielded to the temptation of including a youth in oriental headgear among the characters. The feature of this work lies in the male nudes strewn over the canvas, to the delight of the academicians. The facial expressions, somewhat less than successful, often fall into that sort of affectation defined today as kitsch. Even the Emperor, now grown heavy with the years, has lost his former distinction and romantic stature, and his gesture of consolation appears merely theatrical and meaningless.

"Imagine, within a radius of one league, nine or ten thousand corpses, four or five thousand dead horses, gun fragments and splintered sabers, the earth scattered with bullets, munitions, twenty-four cannons, and, near them, dead cannoneers cut down as they sought to move them, all this against a freezing, snow-blanketed background!" Cited from a Napoleonic war bulletin, this quotation aptly annotates Gros' famous painting dedicated to *Napoleon on the Battlefield of Eylau* (Plate 45). That savage but futile clash costing thousands of lives portended the imminent debacle—the collapse of Bonaparte's dominion. As always, Gros worked from on-the-spot sketches (in this case by Denon himself, who even took the trouble to indicate the prevailing atmospheric conditions on that fatal day), drawing his inspiration from ancient Roman art such as the Ludovisi and other battle sarcophagi in the Museo delle Terme and the Trojan Column to create a deeply moving image of the Emperor, victorious but just and compassionate. His arm raised, his expression mournful, with paternal kindliness he receives the vanquished warriors who prostrate themselves before him. His lips seem to be uttering the famous phrase he pronounced on the occasion of that fearful slaughter, "This is a spectacle meant to inspire princes with the love of peace and the horror of war," an observation that sounds odd from the lips of one of history's most ruthless war-makers. Judged purely as a work of art, Gros' canvas is a masterpiece worthy to hang with *The Plague at Jaffa*; that such was meant to be its destination can, in fact, be proved by its almost identical dimensions. Unquestionably it served as a model for the youthful Géricault, whose splendid officers (Plate 38) clearly reveal a thorough scrutiny of this and other Gros canvases; in *The Wounded Cuirassier* (1814) we behold the catastrophe implied in *The Battlefield of Eylau*. Géricault copied various works of his adored master with such precision that some of his earlier drawings were long attributed to Gros; and we know that he had a small copy of *The Battlefield of Eylau* brought to his deathbed. Yet, despite the honors paid him by the new generation of French painters, years later the aged and embittered Gros still could not grasp the significance of the very revolution he himself had incited. For his dedication to David's classicist doctrine, he renounced his own personality to such an extent that, of Delacroix's *The Massacres at Chios,* he exclaimed, "This is the massacre of painting!" although it virtually pays homage to *The Plague at Jaffa.* This conflict between his true impulses and the course he forced himself to follow drove him in the end to suicide.

Gros' declaration of principles clarifies the difference between David's poetics and his own: "You must look to the whole, the totality of the movement, of the dimensions, of light and shadow, of the overall effect. You must never concern yourself with a single part without considering the whole. Are you tracing the head? Look to the feet!" Thus, David to the contrary, he proclaimed a concept certainly more modern than the master's hedonistic, neoclassic perfectionism.

"Gros lifted everyday subjects to the sublime. He could portray custom, habits, and the passions of our time without ever falling into the petty or trivial," said Eugene Delacroix of his gigantic *The Battle of Abukir* (Plates 35 and 36). Considered one of Gros' masterpieces when it was unveiled, it is so poorly preserved that its merits are difficult to assess. Gros executed the work on commission from Jean-Paul Murat, protagonist of the action, whose tragic fate the painting soon followed into oblivion. When Stendhal chanced to see it in Naples only a few years after the fall of the Empire, it was already in a deplorable condition. But the better-preserved parts of the painting and the overwhelming vision of the whole (Gros undoubtedly used his sketch for *Nazareth* and referred to illustrious models of the past, from Giulio Romano to Le Brun) fully justify the enthusiasm of his contemporaries. With his typically profound critical insight, Delacroix interpreted the work thus: "The pasha's horse struck down...his rage when he realizes his defeat and sees his soldiers routed...the dragoons' swift charge, the ferocious struggle between the Frenchman, exultant in victory, and the Turk, the Arab, the Negro enemy writhing in fury or gnashing his sword that seems aflame under the footfalls of thousands of frantic soldiers...the banners dragged in the dust...all these sweeping, powerful, distressing images afflict the eye of the spirit." Delacroix hailed the steeds as one of the artist's finest achievements and elsewhere compared them with Rubens', observing that Gros infused his horses with greater nobility and passion. A majestic sketch of the pasha's horse (Plate 34) is on exhibit at the Besançon Museum; in the painting, however, the animal, in an agonized spasm, is shown with its head seemingly fused with Murat's torso.

In these battle paintings Gros maintained an admirable control over his emotions and avoided any excesses to which his histrionic subjects might easily have lured him. On the other hand, Girodet, his friend and emulator, took no such pains in *The Revolt of Cairo* (Plate 37). True, the scene is one of horror and gore, but where Gros' approach was always potent but measured, Girodet gave in to the violent, sadistic-masochistic streak in his nature. He was a gifted artist but his aesthetic sense was morbid, obsessive, and given to an affected worship of beauty, and he would concern himself more with some cruel or ghastly detail than with the total interpretation of his theme. Macabre ideas and bloodcurdling touches inflamed his imagination, which, as his master David once acidly remarked, "was sorely bereft of reason." Consequently, the most compelling feature of this work is the turbid agitation of the artist's fantasy. All the same, apart from Gros' representation, it is the only canvas to give us valuable historical insights into the conduct of the fierce, futile battles waged in those years. It is not by chance that *The Revolt of Cairo* lacks a central figure; in the appalling violence that spills over the canvas, the single action most in evidence is that of a young officer dealing a tremendous blow to the kneeling Negro who clasps the nude, muscular leg of an Arab with one hand while, with the other, he holds a severed head, its long, plaited braids scrupulously described. Girodet's taste for crudity, for subtle nuances in his skin textures and fabrics, the dark, ambiguous emotions he portrayed were characteristics that typify the artist and give us enlightening clues into his labyrinthine emotional temperament — a man forever gripped by a tormenting romantic fervor that affected other aspects of his work.

David began *Leonid at Thermopoli* (Plate 56) soon after completing *The Sabine Women*, but finished it years later in 1814, just before the Empire collapsed. While this work is irrelevant to Napoleonic battle painting, it pertains if only as a symbol of Bonaparte's eventual defeat. Almost fifteen years of meditation apparently contributed little of value to the final results; many of the painting's defects can be attributed to conflicting states of mind and antithetical techniques both in the painting and the composition. It must be remembered, however, that David often pressed his pupils into service; therefore many of the ideas incorporated into the work were not his own, even if he did accept them. Since defeat is the theme of the *Leonid,* it displeased the young Napoleon ("Why trouble to paint the conquered?" he asked David), and perhaps this in part explains its outcome. Still, during the One Hundred Days, when the Emperor visited David to see the completed canvas, he gave it his full approval and asked for copies to be hung in the military academies as a moral example for the cadets; the abrupt shift in his political fortunes intervened, however.

Just as *The Sabine Women* symbolized the French national will for peace after so many years of tumultuous uprisings, so did the *Leonid* state David's purpose to commend those who can confront disaster with lofty dignity. Already *démodé* by 1814, it glowed with a lyricism that had little in common with the prevailing style of the new generation or even the artist's own disciples (Géricault exhibited *The Wounded Cuirassier* in the same year), but we should not overlook its historical importance and profound moral significance even if, as

Delécluze pointed out, what David initiated poetically he finished prosaically.

The Ossian Vogue

Napoleon passionately admired James Macpherson, the Scottish Homer of the North, who forged that astonishing literary pastiche in the name of Ossian, a legendary Irish bard of Gaelic literature. This apocryphal work reaped an enormous success and, hastily translated into all languages, exerted a strong influence over the art and literature of all Europe. In 1800, when Percier and Fontaine were furnishing Bonaparte's Malmaison country villa, the general wanted two paintings with an Ossian theme for the gilded salon and awarded the commissions to Gérard and Girodet. In a painting described by a contemporary critic as *piquant d'originalité, heureux de conception et d'exécution*, Gérard grasped the essence of Ossianic poetics in a fairly direct interpretation. Through rarefied transparency, he achieved an icy, phantasmagoric atmosphere that Fontanelle aptly termed *angoisse passionée.* This "passionate anguish," perhaps the artist's finest exploit, must have delighted Napoleon, because, a few years later, he commissioned Isabey to reproduce the work in miniature for his copy of the Ossian saga. It was also much appreciated by other European monarchs for whom Gérard made at least four copies (the original being lost, Plate 46 is a reproduction of the version at Malmaison).

As could be expected, Girodet, eager as ever to flaunt his amazing versatility, gave himself wholly to the task. What emerged was certainly the most involuted painting of the epoch, an incredible tangle of human and animal forms, of light and shade, of the real and fantastic, all confounded in a weird, decorative arabesque—a conceit excessively pretentious even if it possesses genuine poetry. The artist boasted that he had even invented the costumes worn by his mythical characters, but even more surprising than the garments they wear is the casual manner in which he combines them with the uniforms and gaudy headgear of the French generals lost in the first Napoleonic campaigns (Plate 47). A striking facet of Girodet's precious nature is evident in his stubborn insistence on minute detail, which he serves up here in the most refined, unusual guises. "Painting for him seems to be the career of a galley slave," David justly observed. Again, in *The Dying Malvina* (Plate 48), a painting related to the Malmaison work, he repeats his cold but faultless representation of fabrics, of hair, of light glowing on the sculptured, marble breast. We hardly know which to admire most, the elegance of the composition, the pathetic clasping of hands, or the juxtaposition of two such contrasting faces.

Ossian's Dream (Plate 51), painted by Ingres a decade later for Napoleon's bedchamber in the Quirinale Palace in Rome, is explicitly patterned on Gérard's canvas. Both, for instance, place the bard's powerful figure in the foreground. The inspiration for these two works undoubtedly stemmed from a Gros painting, now lost but reproduced by Shlenoff in a drawing in *Ingres, ses sources littéraires,* in which Malvina bends mournfully over the harp she is strumming in much the same pose as Gérard has put Ossian. But apart from this, Ingres held to his concept of the ideal composition—a calm, logical design filled with solid, calibrated forms, including a chorus of translucent figures offering the artist ample opportunity to give full scope to all the delicate subtleties of his palette. (Originally oval, the work was designed to decorate the center of a ceiling.) In its clarity of line it seemed altogether non-Ossian to Van Tieghem in his well-known *Ossian in France*, but that hardly matters because certainly Ingres' painting excels those of his fellow disciples in grandeur and formal solidity. If it lacks Girodet's sophisticated novelty and the vibrant, pastoral beauty of Gérard's masterpiece, it is still vastly impressive in its noble, classic serenity, and it marks a milestone in early nineteenth-century art.

In his *Malvina Dying in Fingal's Arms* and an engraving for Racine's *Phèdre*, Girodet hit upon a remarkable compositional conceit by posing the woman's splendid figure diagonally. This idea must have appealed strongly to Ingres since he appropriated it for his famous *Tu Marcellus Eri,* painted in Rome about 1812 either for an officer of the Imperial Army or the Quirinale Palace (there are several versions; reproduced here is the fine but probably fragmentary Brussels version, Plate 49). But there is a notable difference in the results achieved by two artists spurred by such divergent metaphysical motivations. Girodet solved the problem of artificial light by resorting to neo-Renaissance rationality, while the heroic *preciosité* of the sculptured figures is cast in a solemn, classic plasticity. He gave a truly Piero della Francesca objectivity to the three characters, portrayed with a simplicity so all-embracing and deeply meditated that they seem altogether natural. In this and other compositions on historical, mythological, and religious themes, as well as in his portraits, Ingres "follows the spirit even to the faintest undulations of the epidermis."

The same admirable stylization stamps another Ingres work, *Romulus, Victor of Acrone* (Plate 50), completed in Rome in 1812. Designed as an imposing frieze, this pagan triumph has a frieze-like mood, and its Mantegna quality is enhanced by the use of tempera. The figures for the most part are designed on ancient models, but Ingres, abiding by the primitivist theory to which he then subscribed, gave them an almost bidimensional substance. Acrone's corpse, bleeding on the ground, was modeled on authentic studies from life (one of the drawings is in the Metropolitan Museum). The artist observed the body in various positions, then abstracted it, stripping away the most immediate tactile elements to arrive at an idealization in the manner of a classic bas-relief.

By comparison with the contemporary works of Ingres and those of the young Eugene Delacroix a decade later, this nude figure offers interesting similarities and contrasts. Ironically, *Romulus, Victor* was intended to hang in the second salon of the Palazzo di Monte Cavallo, now known as the Quirinale Palace, but fate decreed that Napoleon was never to install himself in those apartments so sumptuously prepared for him.

16

PLATES

The Portraits

PLATE 1   JACQUES LOUIS DAVID *Napoleon Crossing Mount St. Bernard,* 1800 (271 x 232 cm) Berlin, Charlottenburg, Verwaltung der ehemaligen Staatlichen Schlösser und Gärten

PLATE 2   Jean-Antoine Gros *Bonaparte at Arcole*, 1796 (72 x 59 cm) Paris, Louvre

PLATE 3   JACQUES LOUIS DAVID *Bonaparte as First Consul*, 1797 (81 x 64 cm) Paris, Louvre

PLATE 4   Jean-Dominique Ingres *Bonaparte as First Consul*, 1804 (227 x 147 cm) Liège, Musée des Beaux-Arts

PLATE 5   JACQUES LOUIS DAVID *Napoleon in His Study*, 1812 (203.9 x 125.1 cm) Washington, D. C.,
National Gallery of Art, Samuel H. Kress Collection

PLATE 6   JEAN-DOMINIQUE INGRES *Napoleon I on the Imperial Throne*, 1806 (260 x 163 cm) Paris,
Musée de l'Armée, Palais des Invalides

PLATE 7   JACQUE LOUIS DAVID *Napoleon in Imperial Robes,* 1805 (50 x 41 cm) Lille, Musée des Beaux-Arts

PLATE 8   FRANÇOIS GÉRARD *Marie Louise and the King of Rome*, 1813 (240 x 162 cm) Versailles, Musée

PLATE 9   ANDREA APPIANI *Napoleon,* 1805 (100 x 75 cm) Vienna, Kunsthistorisches Museum (Photo: Meyer)

PLATE 10   JEAN-BAPTISTE WICAR *Julie Bonaparte, Queen of Naples, and Her Daughters,* 1809 (235 x 177 cm) Naples, Capodimonte

PLATE 11 ROBERT LEFÈVRE *Letitia Bonaparte in Court Dress*, 1813, Rome, Museo Napoleonico

PLATE 12   JEAN-ANTOINE GROS *Cristine Boyer, First Wife of Lucien Bonaparte, c.* 1800 (214 x 132 cm)
Paris, Louvre

PLATE 13   PIERRE-PAUL PRUD'HON *The Empress Josephine,* 1805 (244 x 179 cm) Paris, Louvre

PLATE 14   MARIE BENOIST *Marianne Elisa Bonaparte, c.* 1810 (214 x 129 cm) Lucca, Pinacoteca

PLATE 15   FRANÇOIS GÉRARD *Joachim Murat* (218 x 141 cm) Naples, Museo di San Martino

PLATE 16   FRANÇOIS GÉRARD *Portrait of Queen Hortense,* 1805 (65.5 x 54 cm) Arenenberg, Napoleonmuseum

PLATE 17   ANDREA APPIANI *Portrait of Eugène Beauharnais* (15 x 12 cm) Venice, Museo Correr

PLATE 18   GIUSEPPE CAMMARANO *Queen Caroline Dressed as a Neapolitan Peasant*, 1813, Rome, Museo Napoleonico

PLATE 19   JACQUES LOUIS DAVID *The Daughters of Joseph Bonaparte, c.* 1822 (130 x 100 cm) Rome, Museo Napoleonico

PLATE 20   ANNE-LOUIS GIRODET *Portrait of the Baron Dominique Jean Larrey, Surgeon General of the Egyptian Army,* 1804 (65 x 55 cm)
Paris, Louvre

PLATE 21   JACQUES LOUIS DAVID *Portrait of Pope Pius VII*, 1805 (86 x 72 cm) Paris, Louvre

PLATE 22 FRANÇOIS-XAVIER FABRE *Lucien Bonaparte*, Rome, Museo Napoleonico

PLATE 23   JACQUES LOUIS DAVID *Portrait of Comte François de Nantes,* 1811 (114 x 75 cm) Paris,
Musée Jacquemart-André

PLATE 24   ELISABETH VIGÉE-LEBRUN *Portrait of Mme de Staël as Corinna*, 1808 (140 x 118 cm) Geneva, Musée d'Art et d'Histoire

PLATE 25   ANNE-LOUIS GIRODET *Portrait of Chateaubriand,* 1810 (130 x 96 cm) Saint-Malo, Musée

PLATE 26   JEAN-ANTOINE GROS *The Duchess of Angoulême Embarking for Pauillac, April 1, 1815,* 1819 (320 x 504 cm) Bordeaux, Musée des Beaux-Arts

Ceremonies and Battle Scenes

PLATE 27   JACQUES LOUIS DAVID *Emperor Napoleon Crowning the Empress Josephine in the Cathedral of Notre Dame, 1805–1808*
(610 x 931 cm) Paris, Louvre

PLATE 28 JACQUES LOUIS DAVID *Emperor Napoleon Crowning the Empress Josephine in the Cathedral of Notre Dame* (detail), 1805–1808 (610 x 931 cm) Paris, Louvre

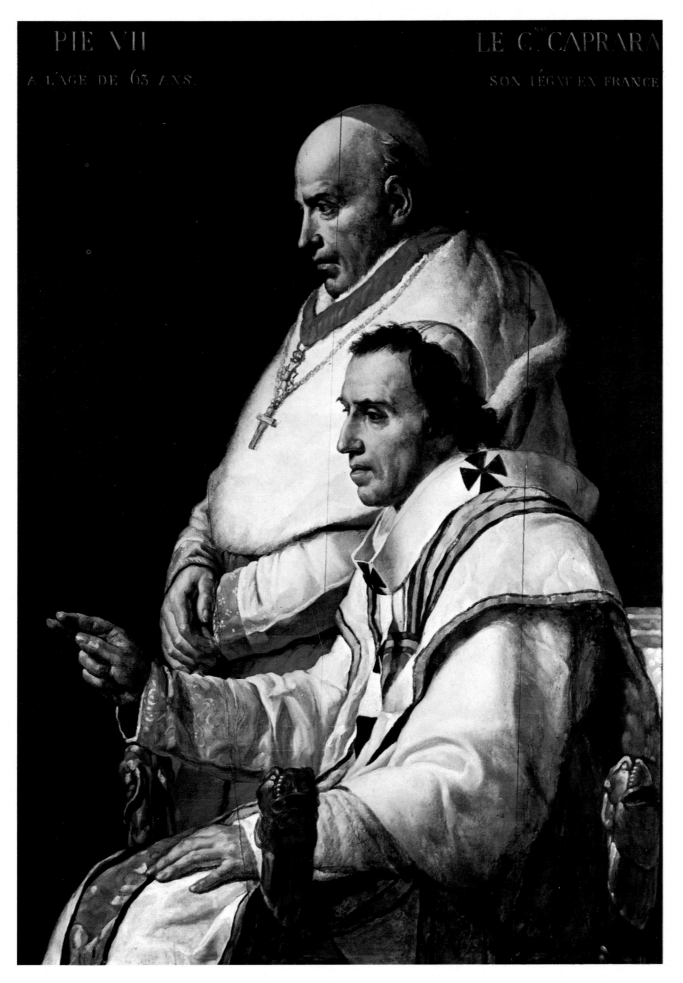

PLATE 29   JACQUES LOUIS DAVID *Pope Pius VII and Cardinal Caprara, c.* 1805 (138.1 x 95.9 cm) Philadelphia, Henry McIlhenny Collection

PLATE 30   JACQUES LOUIS DAVID *The Arrival of Napoleon at the Hôtel-de-Ville, Paris*, 1805 (26.2 x 40.8 cm) Paris, Louvre, Cabinet des Dessins

PLATE 31 JACQUES LOUIS DAVID *The Distribution of the Eagles*, 1808 (18.3 x 29.1 cm) Paris, Louvre, Cabinet des Dessins

PLATE 32   JACQUES LOUIS DAVID *The Oath of the Army to the Emperor after the Distribution of the Eagles on the Champ de Mars, Paris, December 5, 1804* (detail), *1810 (610 x 971 cm) Versailles, Musée*

PLATE 33   JACQUES LOUIS DAVID *The Oath of the Army to the Emperor after the Distribution of the Eagles on the*
Champ de Mars, Paris, December 5, 1804 (detail), 1810 (610 x 971 cm) Versailles, Musée

PLATE 34 JEAN-ANTOINE GROS *The Battle of Nazareth*, 1801 (135 x 195 cm) Nantes, Musée des Beaux-Arts

PLATE 35   JEAN-ANTOINE GROS *Murat Defeating the Egyptian Army in the Battle of Aboukir, July 25, 1799* (detail of Mustapha Pasha), 1806 (578 x 968 cm) Versailles, Musée

PLATE 36   JEAN-ANTOINE GROS *Murat Defeating the Egyptian Army in the Battle of Aboukir, July 25, 1799* (detail of Murat), 1806 (578 x 968 cm) Versailles, Musée

PLATE 37   ANNE-LOUIS GIRODET *The Cairo Rebellion* (detail), 1810 (365 x 500 cm) Versailles, Musée

PLATE 38   THÉODORE GÉRICAULT *Chasseur Officer on Horseback Charging* (53 x 40 cm) Paris, Louvre

PLATE 39   JEAN-ANTOINE GROS *The Horse of Mustapha Pasha* (89 x 175 cm) Besançon, Musée

The Acts of Clemency

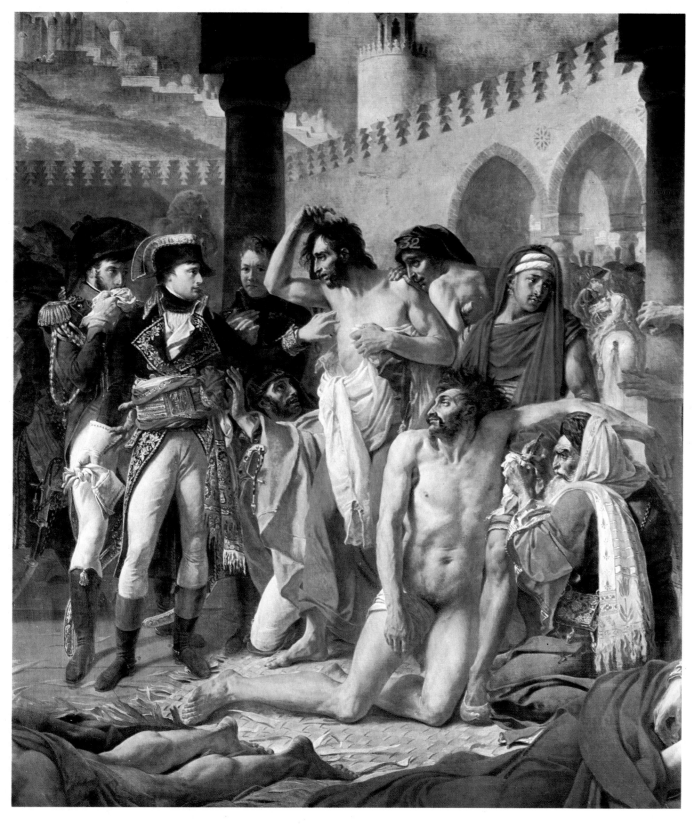

PLATE 40   JEAN-ANTOINE GROS *Bonaparte Visiting the Pesthouse at Jaffa, March 11, 1799* (detail), 1804 (532 x 720 cm)
Paris, Louvre

58

PLATE 41   CHARLES MEYNIER *The Return of Napoleon to the Island of Lobau after the Battle of Essling, May 22, 1809* (detail), 1812 (473 x 529 cm) Versailles, Musée

PLATE 42 · JEAN-ANTOINE GROS *The Surrender of Madrid, December 4, 1808* (detail), 1810 (361 × 500 cm) Versailles, Musée

PLATE 43   Francisco Goya 3 May 1808: The Execution of the Defenders of Madrid (detail), 1814 (266 x 345 cm) Madrid, Museo del Prado

61

PLATE 44   GUILLAUME-FRANÇOIS COLSON *The Entrance of Napoleon into Alexandria, July 3, 1798* (detail), 1812
(365 x 500 cm) Versailles, Musée

PLATE 45   JEAN-ANTOINE GROS *Napoleon on the Battlefield of Eylau, February 9, 1807* (detail), 1808 (533 x 800 cm)
Paris, Louvre

The Ossian Paintings

PLATE 46   FRANÇOIS GÉRARD *The Dream of Ossian*, 1801 (180 x 198 cm) Paris, Musée National de Malmaison

PLATE 47   ANNE-LOUIS GIRODET *Ossian and His Warriors Receiving the Dead Heroes of the French Army*, 1802
(192 x 182 cm) Paris, Musée National de Malmaison

PLATE 48   ANNE-LOUIS GIRODET *Malvina Dying in the Arms of Fingal* (113 x 147 cm) Varzy, Musée

PLATE 49   JEAN-DOMINIQUE INGRES *Virgil Reading from the ''Aeneid'' to Augustus,* 1819 (138 x 142 cm) Brussels, Musées Royaux des Beaux-Arts

PLATE 50 JEAN-DOMINIQUE INGRES *Romulus Conqueror of Acron*, 1812 (276 x 530 cm) Paris, École des Beaux-Arts

PLATE 51 JEAN-DOMINIQUE INGRES *The Dream of Ossian*, 1813 (348 x 275 cm) Montauban, Musée Ingres

PLATE 52   Jean-Dominique Ingres *The Apotheosis of Napoleon I*, 1853 (49 x 49 cm) Paris, Musée Carnavalet

PLATE 53   JEAN-ANTOINE GROS *Study for the cupola of the Panthéon, c.* 1811 (73 x 73 cm) Paris, Musée Carnavalet

PLATE 54   BARTOLOMEO PINELLI *The Goddess Roma and the King of Rome*, 1811, Rome, Museo Napoleonico

PLATE 55   ANDREA APPIANI *The Apotheosis of Napoleon I* (detail), Tremezzo, Villa Carlotta

PLATE 56   JACQUES LOUIS DAVID *Leonidas at Thermopylae,* 1799–1814 (392 x 533 cm) Paris, Louvre

PLATE 57   PIERRE-PAUL PRUD'HON *The Triumph of Bonaparte,* 1800 (97 x 117 cm) Lyons, Musée des Beaux-Arts

PLATE 58   ANTONIO ZUCCARELLI *Portrait of Murat*, Rome, Museo Napoleonico

PLATE 59   JEAN-BAPTISTE ISABEY *Cristine Boyer*, Rome, Museo Napoleonico

PLATE 60   PIERRE-PAUL PRUD'HON *Venus and Adonis*, 1812 (244 x 172 cm) London, Wallace Collection

THE ARTISTS

ANDREA APPIANI

Born May 23, 1754, in Milan. He studied painting with various artists, but his most influential master was the Florentine, Giuliano Traballesi. Except for brief excursions to Florence, Rome, Naples, Parma, and Bologna, he lived most of his life in Milan. He visited Paris and Versailles in 1801, when he was official portrait-artist for the Napoleonic regime in Lombardy, a post he held until 1813.

The foremost examples of his art during this period were his frescoes in the Royal Palace in Milan—*Napoleon's Apotheosis* and thirty-three tempera paintings depicting the new Caesar's major victories. Apart from subjects inspired by the emperor, he also executed several figurations of prominent contemporaries, including a splendid, posthumous portrait of General Desaix, whose death he was likewise to represent on canvas; in fact, he drew a small sketch of this subject in a letter to Gamba in 1800.

Appiani did many drawings of the Imperial family and members of the court, among them the stupendous pencil and watercolor profile of Eugène Beauharnais (reproduced here) taken from Count Cicognara's album and today exhibited in

APPIANI *Napoleon and His Court*, Milan, Accademia di Brera

the Correr Museum in Venice.
He died in Milan, November 8, 1817.

MARIE BENOIST

Marie-Guilhemine de Laville-Leroux was born in 1768 in Paris. She studied with David and with Elisabeth Vigée-Lebrun, whose *Mémoires* mention her with praise. She exhibited at the Salon for the first time in 1791.

Benoist's paintings reveal no exceptional creative originality, but nevertheless she achieved distinction at least twice—in *Portrait of a Negress* (signed and exhibited at the 1800 Salon and now in the Louvre) and in her *Portrait of Elisa Bonaparte*, reproduced here. Until recently, the latter work was attributed to various painters besides Benoist, but discovery of the initials MB in one corner of the canvas definitively resolved the question.

She died in Paris in 1826.

GIUSEPPE CAMMARANO

Born in Sciacca (Agrigento), January 4, 1766. He studied at the Fine Arts Academy in Naples. He was about twenty when he went to Rome with a scholarship from the Neapolitan government. In Caserta he painted decorations in the Palace and Cathedral, where his *Last Supper* is still kept.

DAVID *Self-Portrait*, Florence, Uffizi

In 1817 he painted an *Apotheosis of the Great Poets* and an *Apotheosis of the Bourbon Dynasty* for the San Carlo Theatre in Naples. He was also a portraitist and represented various members of the Bourbon family. Many of his canvases can be seen in the San Martino Museum in Naples.

Cammarano died in Naples, October 8, 1850.

JACQUES LOUIS DAVID

Born in Paris, August 30, 1748, of a modest, bourgeois family. His forebears had been small traders for generations. He was related to François Boucher, a principal painter of the day, and to Desmaisons, a prominent architect. At the time, Rococo art, encouraged by the court and that petticoat Apollo, Madame de Pompadour, was in full flush. Not surprisingly, therefore, David evinced an interest in painting in his early boyhood and decided to devote his time to art.

His mentor was the painter Vien, whose works remind us today of a sort of compromise between vivacious Louis XV décor and the *austère ancien* championed by Cochin and the most advanced coterie of artists.

Emerging onto this motley, cultural scene, David hardly sparkled with skill or originality in his first efforts; not until he went to Rome in 1775 did his neoclassic concept of art mature. Through five years of vastly stimulating exposure both to the new Italian currents and ancient, classic art, he discovered his own true, artistic instinct, which would manifest itself in diverse ways. And if he chose classicism as his genre, he would never forget the examples of the Flemish colorists and Caravaggio realism. Not that contemporary Italian art was by any means exceptional—the outstanding works being Marsiglia's *San Rocco* and Ruffey's *The Bronze Serpent*—but the knowledge he enthusiastically acquired in those years would always be useful to him.

Immediately after his return to France in 1780, the initial result of his new discoveries took form in one of the century's finest portraits, that of *Count Potocki*, in Warsaw, which he had sketched in Naples in 1779.

Several other canvases, such as *Belisario* and *Andromache*, confirmed his fame, which became universal with *The Oath of the Horatii*, painted in Rome in 1784. Of this work Pompeo Batoni exclaimed, "You and I are painters. The others can be pitched into the river." The *Horatii* commenced the era of David's greatest artistic and political glory, which was to endure until Napoleon's defeat in 1815.

DAVID *Napoleon Crowning Himself*, Paris, Louvre, Cabinet des Dessins

DAVID *The Distribution of the Eagles,* Versailles, Musée

Canvases like *Socrates* (1787) and *Brutus* (1789) are intrinsic with the spirit of the Revolution, while *Marat* (1793) is indeed its supreme artistic testimonial.

Jacobin and friend of Robespierre until his fall, David, despite a marked speech defect, played an important role in French public life. He even dared to plead the cause of several colleagues who had fallen into disgrace—among them Fragonard and Hubert Robert.

David was also an ardent Bonapartist. Like many other revolutionaries, he saw in the "French Caesar" the logical consequence of the Revolution and a stalwart barrier against a dreaded return to the *ancien régime*. In paintings that paid lofty tribute to Napoleon's grandeur but not without formidable artistic merit—particularly the *Coronation,* one of the most representative masterpieces of all time—he conferred a distinct, immediately identifiable style on the Empire. With the return of the Bourbons after Waterloo, David went into exile in Brussels, where he remained until his death, staunchly refusing to make any move toward repatriation (although a mere gesture would have brought about his recall).

Although he produced few masterpieces during the ten years he spent in Belgium, David did occasionally paint with his former spirit, as in his portrait of *Count Turenne,* now in Copenhagen.

In Brussels, he relied on his pupils' help to such an extent that paintings like *The Three Women of Gand* (Louvre) cannot be accepted as autographical with any certainty.

He had often turned to others for help—to Ingres in his portrait of Madame Récamier—to Fabre and Girodet, as Rosenblum recently confirmed in the controversial copy of *The Horatii* in Toledo.

David's art, like that of every great artist, still remains an open question. Although the major exponent of neoclassicism, he could still "read" objects (note the workbasket in *Brutus*) and observe nature with an intensity seldom equaled in art. His was a singular blend of reality and the ideal.

David died in Brussels in 1825.

FRANÇOIS-XAVIER FABRE

Born in Montpellier in 1766. Pupil of Vien and later of David, he won the Prix de Rome in 1787. After visiting Rome he went to Florence, and there he became the intimate friend of Vittorio Alfieri and his mistress, the Countess of Albany.

After Alfieri's death, Fabre married the Countess of Albany, who bequeathed her valuable art collection to him. It is now the nucleus of the Montpellier Museum's collection.

The most memorable works of this illustrious portraitist are his figurations of Alfieri and the Countess.

Fabre died in Montpellier in 1837.

GIRODET *Portrait of Gérard*, 1789 (engraving by F. Girard)

FRANÇOIS GÉRARD

Born in Rome in 1770, the son of a French father and Italian mother. At an early age he went to Paris to study with Brenet and later studied with David, who secured him the Prix de Rome after his father's death. In France his career began grimly, but his friendship with the famous miniaturist Isabey soon reaped him many commissions. He painted the *Portrait of Isabey with his Daughter* (Louvre) in 1795, and, in the same year, he painted a *Belisario*. These two works won him widespread recognition.

During the Empire his success was so resounding that he was hailed as the greatest portraitist of the day. Almost every monarch in Europe sought to be painted by Gérard, lauded not without exaggeration as "the painter of kings and the king of painters." But also in his historical works Gérard had moments of soaring inspiration; note *Ossian* (1801, Paris, reproduced in this volume) and *Corinne at Cape Misenum* (1822, Lyons).

Prominent in Parisian social circles, he held a famous salon for many decades. He was appointed royal painter in 1817 and named baron by Louis XVIII in 1819, despite his Bonapartist precedence. His correspondence, published posthumously by his nephew, is thick with fascinating letters from outstanding artists and celebrities of the period. Gérard died in Paris in 1837.

THÉODORE GÉRICAULT

Born in Rouen in 1791 of a well-to-do family. In 1808, he enrolled in Charles Vernet's studio but transferred two years later to Pierre Guérin's tutelage. From both these men he received a some-

what free and varied training—preromantic from the former, classicist and formal from the latter. His idol was Jean-Antoine Gros.

His first famous painting, the *Cavalry Officer of the Imperial Guard*, was exhibited at the 1812 Salon. Of this canvas David exclaimed, "I do not recognize this stroke," a comment intended in the positive sense, notwithstanding the master's diverse concept of art.

Géricault's *Wounded Cuirassier*, exhibited two years later, consolidated his fame. After joining Louis XVIII's musketeers, despite his Bonapartist taint, he went to Rome and painted such important works as his various studies for *The Race of the Berbers*.

In 1819 he painted *The Raft of the Medusa*, a landmark in modern painting. From England he brought back his work, *The Derby at Epsom*, and a number of fine lithographs. After visiting David in exile, he returned to Paris to devote the last years of his short life to his remarkable series on insane people and the powerful studies for a *Traffic in Negro Slaves*.

He died in Paris, January 26, 1824.

ANNE-LOUIS GIRODET DE ROUCY TRIOSON

Born in Montargis in 1767. Girodet was a pupil of David, and in 1789 he won the Prix de Rome after portraying Louis XVI in conventional style. From Italy he sent *The Sleep of Endymion* to the 1793 Salon, revealing an artistic temperament indefinably ambivalent in his art and sentiments; indeed, the curious fusion of classicism and romanticism unveiled in this canvas proved to be one of Girodet's enduring, stylistic traits. Ex-

GIRODET *The Cairo Rebellion*, Versailles, Musée

hibited at the Salon in 1808, *The Funeral of Atala* (Louvre), inspired by Chateaubriand, already bears the stamp of romanticism.

A contrasting facet of the artist's talent comes to light in *Mademoiselle Lange as Danae* (private collection); here the blending of morbid fastidiousness with malice is disconcerting but eminently successful. Other less allegorical portraits, mainly those of the Trisson children (private collection), display a curious affinity with the German romantics. Not prolific but extremely gifted, Girodet painted *The Deluge* (Louvre), shown at the Salon in 1806, which combines, as David pointed out, the bravura of Michelangelo and the grace of Raphael; he also did *Pygmalion and Galatea*, which was exhibited at the 1819 Salon (recently found in the Dampierre Château and shown at the 1967 Girodet exhibit in Montargis) and a true tour de force of skill and a refined synthesis of the artist's dazzling virtuosity.

A sometime poet and deeply sensitive illustrator of literary works, Girodet struck the ideal vein of his inspiration in his exquisite engravings for the publisher Didot's *Racine*, realized with the collaboration of François Gérard and Pierre-Paul Prud'hon.

He died in Paris, December 8, 1824.

JEAN-ANTOINE GROS

Born in Paris in 1771. He was a pupil of David and remained dedicated to him throughout his life.

Gros *Self-Portrait at the Age of Twenty*, 1791, Toulouse, Musée

When he was suspected of fealty to the *ancien régime*, David procured for him a passport for Italy. He lived mostly in Genoa and Milan where he met the Bonapartes. Josephine assigned him a room in the Serbelloni Palace, in which he portrayed the young general as he sat impatiently on his wife's knees; he produced the renowned *Napoleon at the Battle of Arcola* (1796), and the sketch is reproduced in this volume (both in the Louvre).

In Genoa he studied in depth the art of Rubens, whose example his creative nature urged him to follow against David's classicist precepts. This conflict between vocation and doctrine became more intense when his revered master went into exile and left his studio to Gros.

Although he was officially acclaimed and re-

INGRES *The Family of Lucien Bonaparte*, 1815,
Cambridge, Mass., Harvard University,
Fogg Art Museum

warded with the title of baron after he completed
the Panthéon cupola, his life henceforth was
plagued by a gnawing frustration, and his output,
except for a few superb portraits, declined sharply.
Gros' true genius found its greatest expression in
glorifying Napoleon's feats. As Guizot observed in
1810, "There is no triviality, frigidity, or staginess
in Gros; his genius is best suited to patriotic subjects." The artist committed suicide at Bas-Meudon
(Seine-et-Oise), June 26, 1835.

JEAN-AUGUSTE-DOMINIQUE INGRES

Born at Montauban (Toulouse), August 29, 1780.
Ingres was the son of a humble painter-decorator,
from whom he learned the rudiments of art before
entering David's studio in Paris.

In 1801 he won the Prix de Rome with a work
that represented the arrival of Agamemnon's am-
bassadors in the tent of Achilles, but not until
1806 did he transfer to Rome, which became his
second home after painting several brilliant works,
among them the two portraits of Bonaparte reproduced here. In Rome he immersed himself in the

cult of Raphael, whom he deemed the greatest
painter of all time. While many of his works are
considered masterpieces today, his was a hard
life and he was compelled to draw or paint tourists
and foreigners, producing a number of portraits
now ranked as classics. In 1824, he finally returned
to Paris to receive his first official recognition for
his *Vow of Louis XIII* (Louvre).

In 1826–27 he painted *The Apotheosis of Homer*,
eulogized by Delécluze as the crowning achieve-
ment of the Davidian school.

Again in 1835 he went to Rome as director of
the French Academy at the Villa Medici, but he
returned to France permanently in 1841. Several
honors and commissions awaited him.

True to his instincts until death, he re-created
and repeated subjects he had already painted in
his youth, but he never lost his lyrical touch. A
superior draughtsman and colorist, he invented a
whole universe of the imagination that had nothing to fear from comparison with the triumphant
art of those two giants, David and Delacroix, the
master he both loved and hated and the rival he
execrated.

He died in Paris, January 14, 1867.

JEAN-BAPTISTE ISABEY

Born in Nancy in 1757. He went to Paris in 1785

and studied with David. He secured introductions into court circles and there won recognition as a miniaturist.

During the Revolution he portrayed members of the Convention and formed close ties with Madame de Staël, Madame Récamier, and the young Bonaparte couple. This latter friendship brought him valuable rewards during the Empire, when he became drawing master first to Hortense and Eugène Beauharnais and later to the empress Marie Louise.

His talents, however, were diverse. He planned the elaborate program for Napoleon's coronation and organized many Imperial festivities. He also decorated Sèvres porcelain.

Under the Restoration he was briefly suspected of hostility toward the regime but, once cleared, he was entrusted with important commissions by Louis XVIII, Charles X, Louis Philippe, and, later, by Napoleon III.

He ranks as the reigning miniaturist of his age and one of the greatest in all history.

He died in Paris, April 18, 1855.

ROBERT LEFÈVRE

Born in Bayeux, September 24, 1755. His love for

painting brought him to Paris, where he studied with Regnault and won his recognition primarily as a portraitist.

Landon qualified his contribution to the 1810 Salon as having "great truth in likeness, a broad stroke, a solid polychromy and that vigorous impression of relief that paintings more scrupulously executed cannot always claim." He was court painter to Louis XVIII.

He died in Paris, October 3, 1830.

CHARLES MEYNIER

Born in Paris, November 25, 1768.

A pupil of Vincent, he won the Prix de Rome in 1789, together with Girodet; he later won approval for his exhibits at the Salon in 1800, 1801, and particularly in 1810, with the work reproduced here. He continued to exhibit successfully at the Salon until 1824.

Meynier entered the *Napoleon on the Battlefield at Eylau* competition, which Gros won. The Meynier sketch of this subject is now in the Versailles Museum.

He was a member of the Institute during the One Hundred Days.

He died in Paris, September 6, 1832.

BARTOLOMEO PINELLI

Born in Rome, November 20, 1781.

MEYNIER *The Return of Napoleon to the Island of Lobau*, Versailles, Musée

He was one of his native city's most devoted champions during the cultural movement led by the poet G. Belli.

His scenes of everyday life, drawn or engraved with a captivating spirit, spread his fame over half of Europe.

Apart from this folk art, another aspect of his talent was wholly and inevitably dedicated to neoclassicism. He illustrated many albums and books, evoking with variable faithfulness diverse aspects of the ancient world and the vanished splendors of the Eternal City.

In this vein he painted the court allegory of *The Goddess of Rome and The King of Rome,* reproduced in this volume, and the little-known *Napoleon's War in Spain.*

He died in Rome on April 1, 1835.

PIERRE-PAUL PRUD'HON

Born in Cluny in 1758. After a childhood of misery and privation, he moved to Paris in 1780, where he struggled to earn his living. He then spent several years in Rome and returned to Paris in the crucial year of 1789, but he withdrew to the provinces to wait at length until the storm passed. During this time he was already drawing delicate illustrations for the publisher Didot, displaying a sensitivity that reverted back to the eighteenth century but imbued with a lifelike fragility unknown to contemporary French painting. He was strongly influenced by some of the great Renaissance artists, from Coreggio to Leonardo.

Subsequently he dedicated his art to the Bonapartes and designed a series of decorations for their residence. He portrayed the empress Josephine and later became drawing master to Marie Louise.

As a decorative artist he also designed furniture and other works of art for the Imperial family household. His historical representations were highly successful as, for example, the famous *Justice and Divine Revenge Persecute Crime,* exhibited in the 1808 Salon (now in the Louvre).

Gifted with a singular, psychological insight and a mellow but passionate brushstroke, Prud'hon also painted veritable masterpieces of portraiture. But the scope of his genius is most clearly evident in his exquisite, erotic allegories. In such works as *The Rape of Psyche* (1808, Louvre), he revived early eighteenth-century gracefulness

PRUD'HON *The King of Rome,* 1811

more or less covertly opposed Napoleonic domination.

With the Restoration came fresh honors and new commissions, but her genuine, lyrical vein had by then been exhausted.

She died in Paris in 1842.

JEAN-BAPTISTE WICAR

Born in Lille in 1762. He accompanied David, his master, to Rome and subsequently lived for long periods in Italy.

Here he drew, and later engraved, illustrations for various volumes reproducing the most famous works of art preserved in the Pitti Palace in Florence. He was most interested in ancient art and became an authoritative collector; his priceless collection is now exhibited in the museum in his native city.

A rabid revolutionary, he served on the commission that selected the works of art to be transferred to Paris. Known primarily as a portraitist, he was a member of the San Luca Academy in Rome and director of the Naples Academy.

Wicar died in Rome in 1834.

WICAR *Julie Bonaparte, Queen of Naples*, 1808, Rome, Museo Napoleonico

VIGÉE-LEBRUN *Self-Portrait*, Florence, Uffizi

in a period given to the zealous cult of antiquity.

He died in Paris on February 16, 1823.

ELISABETH VIGÉE-LEBRUN

Born in Paris in 1755. She turned to painting at an early age, and, while still very young, she married an art dealer who was prominent during the last years of the *ancien régime*. Before long she became a favorite of the aristocracy and, eventually, Marie Antoinette's official portraitist.

These were her happiest years. With the Revolution in full tide, she left France in 1789 to make an extended pilgrimage to the courts of Europe — Turin, Rome, Naples, Vienna, Dresden, Berlin, and St. Petersburg, where she lived for some years, returning to Paris in 1802. Her talent was still esteemed, but Napoleon's Paris no longer offered the same brilliant life that had inspired her best canvases. Although she did not disdain to portray members of the Imperial family, including Queen Caroline, she remained loyal to the Bourbon dynasty and to those like herself who

List of Illustrations

Page 19   JACQUES LOUIS DAVID *Napoleon Crossing Mount St. Bernard,* 1800, Berlin, Charlottenburg, Verwaltung der ehemaligen Staatlichen Schlösser und Gärten

20   JEAN-ANTOINE GROS *Bonaparte at Arcole,* 1796, Paris, Louvre

21   JACQUES LOUIS DAVID *Bonaparte as First Consul,* 1797, Paris, Louvre

22   JEAN-DOMINIQUE INGRES *Bonaparte as First Consul,* 1804, Liège, Musée des Beaux-Arts

23   JACQUES LOUIS DAVID *Napoleon in His Study,* 1812, Washington, D. C., National Gallery of Art, Samuel H. Kress Collection

24   JEAN-DOMINIQUE INGRES *Napoleon I on the Imperial Throne,* 1806, Paris, Musée de l'Armée, Palais des Invalides

25   JACQUE LOUIS DAVID *Napoleon in Imperial Robes,* 1805, Lille, Musée des Beaux-Arts

26   FRANÇOIS GÉRARD *Marie Louise and the King of Rome,* 1813, Versailles, Musée

27   ANDREA APPIANI *Napoleon,* 1805, Vienna, Kunsthistorisches Museum (Photo: Meyer)

28   JEAN-BAPTISTE WICAR *Julie Bonaparte, Queen of Naples, and Her Daughters,* 1809, Naples, Capodimonte

29   ROBERT LEFÈVRE *Letitia Bonaparte in Court Dress,* 1813, Rome, Museo Napoleonico

30   JEAN-ANTOINE GROS *Cristine Boyer, First Wife of Lucien Bonaparte, c.* 1800, Paris, Louvre

31   PIERRE-PAUL PRUD'HON *The Empress Josephine,* 1805, Paris, Louvre

32   MARIE BENOIST *Marianne Elisa Bonaparte, c.* 1810, Lucca, Pinacoteca

33   FRANÇOIS GÉRARD *Joachim Murat,* Naples, Museo di San Martino

34   FRANÇOIS GÉRARD *Portrait of Queen Hortense,* 1805, Arenenberg, Napoleonmuseum

35   ANDREA APPIANI *Portrait of Eugène Beauharnais,* Venice, Museo Correr

36   GIUSEPPE CAMMARANO *Queen Caroline Dressed as a Neapolitan Peasant,* 1813, Rome, Museo Napoleonico

37   JACQUES LOUIS DAVID *The Daughters of Joseph Bonaparte, c.* 1822, Rome, Museo Napoleonico

38   ANNE-LOUIS GIRODET *Portrait of the Baron Dominique Jean Larrey, Surgeon General of the Egyptian Army,* 1804, Paris, Louvre

39   JACQUES LOUIS DAVID *Portrait of Pope Pius VII,* 1805, Paris, Louvre

40   FRANÇOIS-XAVIER FABRE *Lucien Bonaparte,* Rome, Museo Napoleonico

41   JACQUES LOUIS DAVID *Portrait of Comte François de Nantes,* 1811, Paris, Musée Jacquemart-André

42   ELISABETH VIGÉE-LEBRUN *Portrait of Mme de Staël as Corinna,* 1808, Geneva, Musée d'Art et d'Histoire

43   ANNE-LOUIS GIRODET *Portrait of Chateaubriand,* 1810, Saint-Malo, Musée

44   JEAN-ANTOINE GROS *The Duchess of Angoulême Embarking for Pauillac, April 1, 1815,* 1819, Bordeaux, Musée des Beaux-Arts

45   JACQUES LOUIS DAVID *Emperor Napoleon Crowning the Empress Josephine in the Cathedral of Notre Dame,* 1805–1808, Paris, Louvre

46   JACQUES LOUIS DAVID *Emperor Napoleon Crowning the Empress Josephine in the Cathedral of Notre Dame* (detail), 1805–1808, Paris, Louvre

47   JACQUES LOUIS DAVID *Pope Pius VII and Cardinal Caprara, c.* 1805, Philadelphia, Henry McIlhenny Collection

48   JACQUES LOUIS DAVID *The Arrival of Napoleon at the Hôtel-de-Ville, Paris,* 1805, Paris, Louvre, Cabinet des Dessins

49   JACQUES LOUIS DAVID *The Distribution of the Eagles,* 1808, Paris, Louvre, Cabinet des Dessins

Page 50   JACQUES LOUIS DAVID *The Oath of the Army to the Emperor after the Distribution of the Eagles on the Champ de Mars, Paris, December 5, 1804* (detail), 1810, Versailles, Musée

51   JACQUES LOUIS DAVID *The Oath of the Army to the Emperor after the Distribution of the Eagles on the Champ de Mars, Paris, December 5, 1804* (detail), 1810, Versailles, Musée

52   JEAN-ANTOINE GROS *The Battle of Nazareth*, 1810, Nantes, Musée des Beaux-Arts

53   JEAN-ANTOINE GROS *Murat Defeating the Egyptian Army in the Battle of Aboukir, July 25, 1799* (detail of Mustapha Pasha), 1806, Versailles, Musée

54   JEAN-ANTOINE GROS *Murat Defeating the Egyptian Army in the Battle of Aboukir, July 25, 1799* (detail of Murat), 1806, Versailles, Musée

55   ANNE-LOUIS GIRODET *The Cairo Rebellion* (detail), 1810, Versailles, Musée

56   THÉODORE GÉRICAULT *Chasseur Officer on Horseback Charging*, Paris, Louvre

57   JEAN-ANTOINE GROS *The Horse of Mustapha Pasha*, Besançon, Musée

58   JEAN-ANTOINE GROS *Bonaparte Visiting the Pesthouse at Jaffa, March 11, 1799* (detail), 1804, Paris, Louvre

59   CHARLES MEYNIER *The Return of Napoleon to the Island of Lobau after the Battle of Essling, May 22, 1809* (detail), 1812, Versailles, Musée

60   JEAN-ANTOINE GROS *The Surrender of Madrid, December 4, 1808* (detail), 1810, Versailles, Musée

61   FRANCISCO GOYA *3 May 1808: The Execution of the Defenders of Madrid* (detail), 1814, Madrid, Museo del Prado

62   GUILLAUME-FRANÇOIS COLSON *The Entrance of Napoleon into Alexandria, July 3, 1798* (detail), 1812, Versailles, Musée

63   JEAN-ANTOINE GROS *Napoleon on the Battlefield of Eylau, February 9, 1807* (detail), 1808, Paris, Louvre

64   FRANÇOIS GÉRARD *The Dream of Ossian*, 1801, Paris, Musée National de Malmaison

65   ANNE-LOUIS GIRODET *Ossian and His Warriors Receiving the Dead Heroes of the French Army*, 1802, Paris, Musée National de Malmaison

66   ANNE-LOUIS GIRODET *Malvina Dying in the Arms of Fingal*, Varzy, Musée

67   JEAN-DOMINIQUE INGRES *Virgil Reading from the "Aeneid" to Augustus*, 1819, Brussels, Musées Royaux des Beaux-Arts

68   JEAN-DOMINIQUE INGRES *Romulus Conqueror of Acron*, 1812, Paris, École des Beaux-Arts

69   JEAN-DOMINIQUE INGRES *The Dream of Ossian*, 1813, Montauban, Musée Ingres

70   JEAN-DOMINIQUE INGRES *The Apotheosis of Napoleon I*, 1853, Paris, Musée Carnavalet

71   JEAN-ANTOINE GROS *Study for the cupola of the Panthéon, c. 1811*, Paris, Musée Carnavalet

72   BARTOLOMEO PINELLI *The Goddess Roma and the King of Rome*, 1811, Rome, Museo Napoleonico

73   ANDREA APPIANI *The Apotheosis of Napoleon I* (detail), Tremezzo, Villa Carlotta

74   JACQUES LOUIS DAVID *Leonidas at Thermopylae*, 1799–1814, Paris, Louvre

75   PIERRE-PAUL PRUD'HON *The Triumph of Bonaparte*, 1800, Lyons, Musée des Beaux-Arts

76   ANTONIO ZUCCARELLI *Portrait of Murat*, Rome, Museo Napoleonico

77   JEAN-BAPTISTE ISABEY *Cristine Boyer*, Rome, Museo Napoleonico

78   PIERRE-PAUL PRUD'HON *Venus and Adonis*, 1812, London, Wallace Collection

The text is based on the Italian original by A. Gonzales Palacios who has also chosen the illustrations.

Translated by William Packer